THE OFFICIAL EXCEPTIONS TO THE RULES OF GOLF

Special Titanium Edition

OTHER GOLF BOOKS BY HENRY BEARD

Mulligan's Laws

Golfing: A Duffer's Dictionary

Leslie Nielsen's Stupid Little Golf Book
(with Leslie Nielsen)

Leslie Nielsen's Bad Golf My Way
(with Leslie Nielsen)

Also By Henry Beard

Zen for Cats

French for Cats

Poetry for Cats

Latin for All Occasions

Latin for Even More Occasions

O.J.'s Legal Pad (with John Boswell)

The Official Politically Correct Dictionary and Handbook
(with Christopher Cerf)

The Official Sexually Correct Dictionary and Handbook
(with Christopher Cerf)

THE OFFICIAL
EXCEPTIONS
TO THE RULES OF
GOLF

SPECIAL TITANIUM EDITION

Henry Beard

HarperCollinsPublishers

HarperCollins*Publishers*
77–85 Fulham Palace Road,
Hammersmith, London W6 8JB
http://www.harpercollins.co.uk

An earlier edition of this book was first published by Grafton,
a division of HarperCollins*Publishers* in 1992, and by
HarperCollins*Publishers* in 1994

This revised edition 1998
1 3 5 7 9 8 6 4 2

A catalogue record for this book is
available from the British Library

ISBN 0 00 653080 X

Printed and bound in Great Britain by Caledonian International
Book Manufacturing Ltd, Glasgow

Contents

IN A HAZARD

Introduction

How many times has this happened to you? Your tee shot takes a bad bounce into rough thick enough to smother a buffalo, or you split the fairway with a perfect 250-yard drive, only to find that it came to rest in a divot hole so deep that if it were on the moon someone would give it a Latin name. Naturally, you tap your ball out of those ridiculous lies and onto a nearby stretch of reasonably playable turf where you have at least a fighting chance of hitting a halfway decent shot.

After all, this isn't the Masters—it's just a friendly game of golf. And anyway, you know perfectly well that your playing partners in the opposite rough and on the other side of the fairway are doing exactly the same thing you are. Why then do you feel this nagging sense of guilt for simply having corrected what is obviously a totally unfair playing condition?

Why? Well, every golfer knows the answer to that question. It's all because of a deadly little booklet called "The Rules of Golf"—over a hundred brain-numbing pages filled with batty commandments, nitpicking definitions, idiotic distinctions, and blatant contradictions, which, taken as a whole, are about as relevant to the game of golf that most people actually play as Escoffier's classic haute cuisine recipes are to microwave cookery.

You see, "The Rules of Golf" as they now stand (and they have been much amended over the years) have come to serve only one real purpose, and that purpose is *not* to establish a universal standard of fair play and sportsmanship for golfers of varying skills anywhere in the world. No, the purpose of "The Rules of Golf" is to ensure that during the opening round of a multimillion-dollar tournament, a modern professional golfer with a bag full of custom-made, individually swing-weighted clubs, the build of a line-backer, the concentration of a mongoose, and a close personal relationship with God, cannot step out onto a lush, manicured, overwatered, rarely played, divot-free, lovingly maintained sod farm of a golf course, like Augusta National, and score a 21-under par on the first 18 holes.

Now, you've seen pros like that on TV complaining about some course you'd kill to play on. And when they bitch and moan because the fairways haven't been cut close enough to let their drives carry 300 yards, or because the stuff in the bunkers isn't actual jewelers' pumice so they can't put a sand wedge a foot from the cup, or because they had to settle for a couple of 2-putts on greens with their own zip codes due to a spike mark or two, you must sometimes say to yourself, "Hey, I'm not playing the same game these guys are."

Well, you're right. You're not. And so it also stands to reason that you shouldn't be playing by *their* rules either. You should be playing by *your* rules—hackers' rules—or, as they are more formally known, "The Official Exceptions to the Rules of Golf."

Most golfers know a handful of these unwritten but customary exceptions—the mulligan, winter rules, gimmes—but the book you are now holding represents the first serious effort to collect and codify in one handy, easy-to-use volume *all 62* of the time-honored, generally recognized modifications of, and exemptions from, "The Rules of Golf." Each exception has been rendered into precise, quotable prose, illustrated with simple-to-understand drawings describing the particular extenuating circumstances the exception covers, and presented in the natural order of play from tee to green so that the appropriate remedy for any situation is always right at your fingertips.

So now it's up to you. Are you going to play the game as it was originally played and was always meant to be played, with a little common sense based on the simple fact that just hitting the ball is hard enough already, so players are entitled to a break once in a while? Or are you going to follow a set of hairsplitting rules drafted by a bunch of fussbudget country club WASPs who think that a municipal course is a period during which one studies tax-free bond issues, whose idea of fun is serving on a committee trying to decide whether a meteorite is a loose impediment or an outside agency, and who basically regard the game of golf not as an enjoyable pastime, but rather as a form of protracted litigation undertaken outdoors?

P.S. They also think that blushing pink and lime green are complementary colors.

Happy hacking.

ON THE
TEE

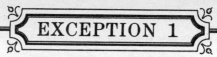
Revisional Ball
(Mulligan)

If, prior to teeing off from the teeing ground of the first hole of any stipulated round, a player informs his fellow players of his intention of replaying one unsatisfactory tee shot and secures from them their clearly stated consent to this procedure, he may, upon hitting a flawed drive, put into play a revisional ball (mulligan) without assessing a stroke or incurring any penalty, under whichever of the following conditions of permissible replay has been mutually agreed to:

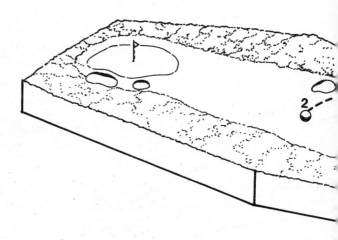

1. On the first tee of any 9-hole or 18-hole course, *or*

2. On the first and the tenth tees of any 18-hole course having two distinct 9-hole layouts, provided play is suspended, however briefly and for whatever purpose, at the conclusion of play on the first 9 holes, *or*

3. On the tee of any one hole, regardless of its position in the sequence of holes.

However, if a player elects to hit a revisional ball, he must play that ball, even if it comes to rest in a lie substantially worse than that occupied by his original ball, unless the option of playing the better of the two balls has itself also been separately endorsed by all the players in the playing group (see: Exception 2, Preferential Ball).

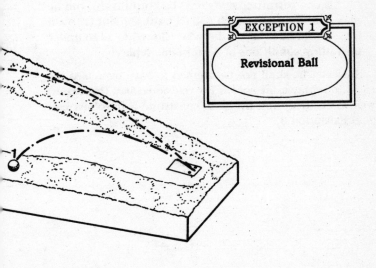

EXCEPTION 1

Revisional Ball

Preferential Ball
(Choosies)

If, after establishing by common consent the right of replay of a drive at a specified point or points during a round, a group of players additionally agree among themselves to allow a right of preference as to play of the first or second ball, a player who has hit a revisional ball (mulligan) following an unsatisfactory tee shot shall have the option of playing either ball, subject to the following restrictions:

1. Before leaving the teeing ground, he must designate which of the two balls he will keep in play, and he may not later amend or alter his decision if it thereafter proves to have been imprudent.

2. If he chooses to keep his original ball in play and pick up his second ball, he shall nevertheless be deemed to have hit his one permitted revisional ball (mulligan), and he may not hit another such ball on a subsequent tee even if he would have been otherwise allowed to do so under prevailing conditions of permissible replay.

However, he shall not be deemed to have exercised his right to replay a tee shot if his revisional ball (mulligan) was so absurdly mis-hit as to constitute a frivolous ball (see: Exception 3).

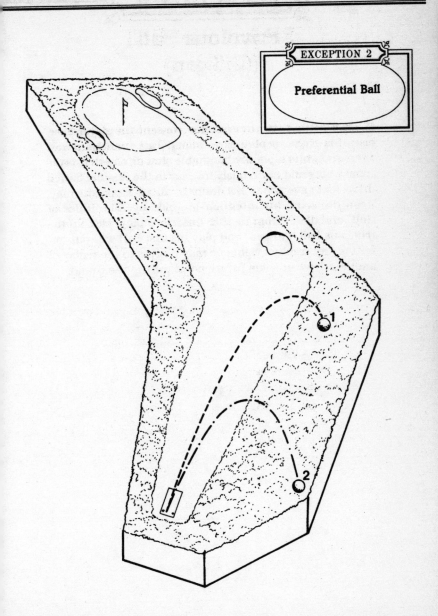

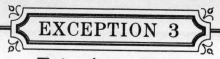

Frivolous Ball
(Gilligan)

If, after hitting an unsatisfactory tee shot, a player exercises his right to play a revisional ball (mulligan) and thereupon hits a plainly laughable shot or one that is demonstrably and ludicrously inferior to the original flawed drive that gave rise to his desire to take a replay, he may, upon declaring his intention to abide by "The Rules of Golf" and desist from further unserious play, pick up the frivolous ball (gilligan) and play his first ball without forfeiting any residual rights he may possess to the replay of another drive at some future point during the round.

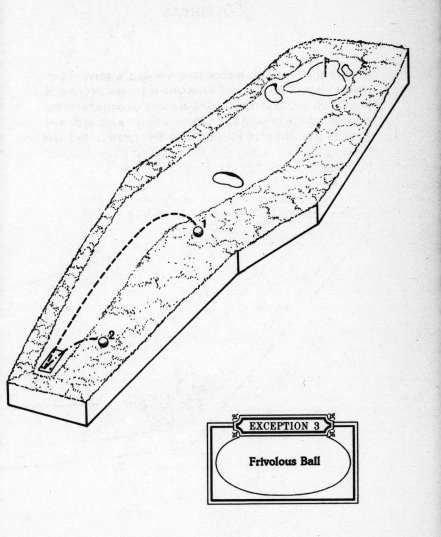

EXCEPTION 3

Frivolous Ball

EXCEPTION 4

Ball Hit Perfectly Straight
(Corrigan)

If, in fairly taking his stance on the teeing ground of any hole, a player intentionally lines up well to the left or well to the right of his desired target in order to compensate for a chronic hook or slice and proceeds to hit a straight and flawless shot directly into unplayable terrain along the

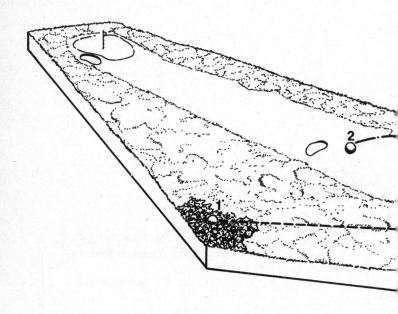

margins of the hole, he may replay that shot without assessing a stroke or incurring any penalty. However, if he thereupon deliberately readjusts his customary corrective alignment to a square stance in the belief that his long-established directional error has been unexpectedly and inexplicably cured, and then hooks or slices his second ball, he must play that shot from wherever it lies, no matter how unfavorable its position, even if he can clearly and convincingly demonstrate to his fellow players that if he had adopted his habitual preventive posture, his ball would have come to rest in the middle of the fairway.

EXCEPTION 4

Ball Hit
Perfectly Straight

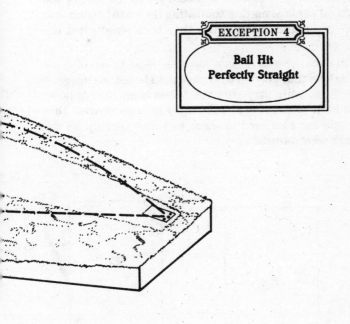

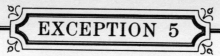
Ball Teed Up
Ahead of the Markers
(Moochies)

A player is permitted to tee up his ball in front of the tee markers defining the forward limits of the teeing ground as follows:

1. If the encroachment is so slight that a complaint about the transgression voiced by another player would constitute an instance of unsportsmanlike conduct considerably more grave than the infraction itself

2. If the markers have been placed far to the rear of the official yardage marker indicating the stated distance to the green and the hole has thus been lengthened improperly

3. If the markers have been placed so close to the blue tee markers that players who have not elected to engage in championship play are nonetheless compelled to do so without even being able to enjoy the approbation that would have accrued to them had they teed up on the back tees voluntarily

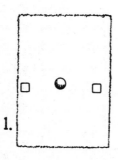

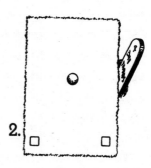

4. If the markers have recently been moved back from a significantly more advanced position and a player is thus being arbitrarily penalized by being denied the opportunity to play the hole from an advantageous tee placement that countless other golfers were permitted to use

5. If the turf within the area of the designated teeing ground has been so damaged by the taking of divots that in teeing up his ball slightly in front of the markers a player merely rectifies an unfair playing condition, and the tiny real advantage he thereby gains is more than offset by the huge potential disadvantage he would have suffered had he been obliged to tee up on the remaining playable turf well to the rear of the markers.

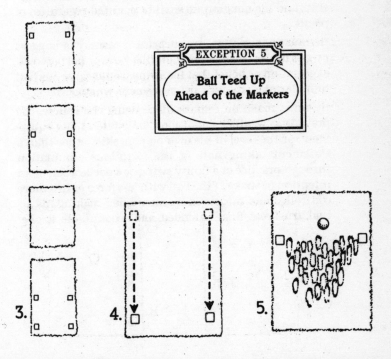

EXCEPTION 5

Ball Teed Up
Ahead of the Markers

3.

4.

5.

EXCEPTION 6

Ball Swung at and Missed
(Practice Swing)

A player who assumes his stance, formally addresses the ball, and then fairly strikes at it, but in so doing fails completely to make contact with any part of the ball, is deemed to have performed a full-address rehearsal of his swing (practice swing) and therefore need *not* count a stroke provided that he strictly observes the following procedure:

1. He must immediately readdress the ball with the same club, and his next stroke shall be counted regardless of result.

2. He must not exhibit any surprise or dismay or suggest by gesture or facial expression that he ever harbored an expectation or belief that his swing would cause his ball to undertake any forward movement whatsoever.

3. He must make no remark disparaging the course, the prevailing weather conditions, the state of his equipment, or the level of his own playing skill, other than a statement taking note of the fortuitous elimination through practice of a faulty swing or a declaration of an intention to strike at the ball with less force or in a more controlled and measured manner when making his actual, true, real, final, intended, and accountable stroke.

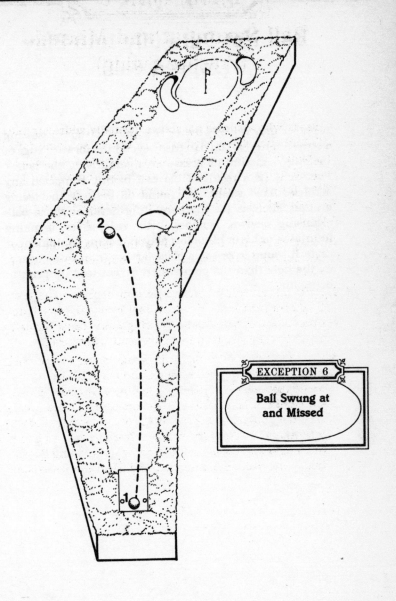

EXCEPTION 6

Ball Swung at
and Missed

EXCEPTION 7

Ball Not Put Fully into Play
(Topped Ball)

A player may replay any tee shot once, without assessing a stroke, if his ball fails to pass beyond the forward edge of the raised mound or grassy area comprising the ladies' tees, or if, as a result of his ball having contacted any artificial fixed equipment found on or near the teeing ground, such as tee markers, informational signs, ball-cleansing devices, benches, litter receptacles, drinking fountains, or his or his fellow players' golfing equipment or carts, it comes to rest in a place farther from, or no nearer to, the hole than the point where it was teed up prior to being hit.

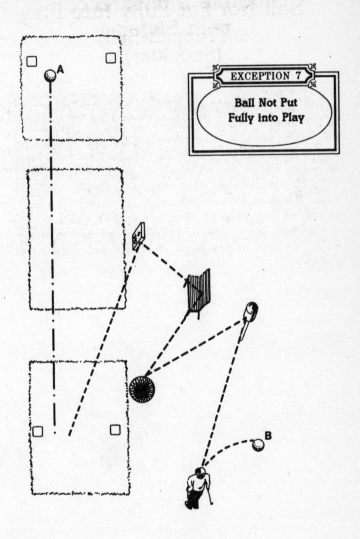

EXCEPTION 8

Audible Interference with Swing
(Spookies)

A player may replay his shot without assessing a stroke if at any time during his backswing or downswing, and prior to the moment when he strikes his ball, he shall hear a distracting sound or noise, including, but not limited to *(a)* a horn, siren, bell, gong, or chime; *(b)* a backfire, tire squeal, or engine whine; *(c)* a cheer, shout, groan, or whoop; *(d)* a bang, clap, crack, crash, slam, or snap; *(e)* a blast, rumble, or roar; *(f)* a thud, click, clunk, rattle, or clatter; *(g)* a bark, bellow, whinny, bleat, or howl; *(h)* a squawk, quack, cackle, cluck, chirp, honk, mew, or coo; *(i)* a cough, hiccup, sniffle, snort, or sneeze; or *(j)* a giggle, chuckle, chortle, snicker, or guffaw.

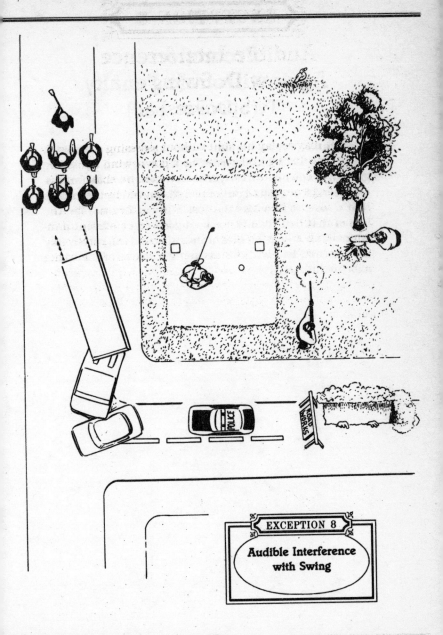

EXCEPTION 8

Audible Interference
with Swing

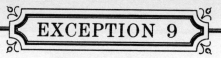

Protection
Against Double Penalty
(Two-Dollar Ball)

If a brand-new, high-quality ball just removed from a sleeve, box, or carton is struck by a player from the teeing ground of any hole directly into water, deep woods, impassable terrain, or ground out-of-bounds under circumstances that appear to foreclose the possibility of its recovery, the loss of that ball shall be deemed good and sufficient punishment for any infraction of the rules, and the player may hit a second ball without assessing a stroke or incurring any further penalty.

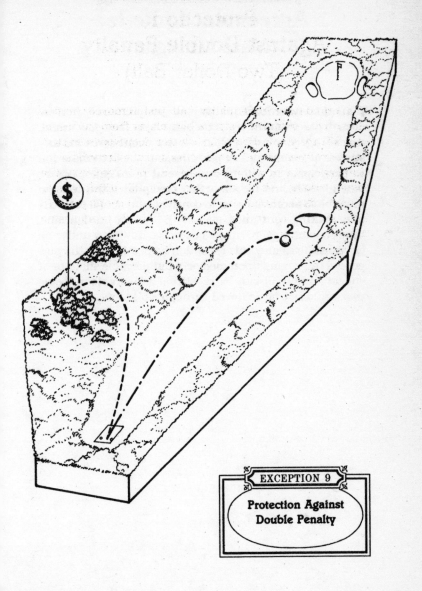

EXCEPTION 9

**Protection Against
Double Penalty**

EXCEPTION 10

Agreement to Re-tee
(Mass Mulligan)

If all of the members of a playing group hit truly horrendous drives from the tee of the same hole, they may unanimously agree to replay their shots without assessing any strokes or incurring any penalties, but the determination to participate in a joint and several re-tee must not be taken lightly, and the shots that precipitated the decision must be so abominable as to constitute an actual catastrophe, making continued play of the hole a burdensome, time-consuming, or fruitless exercise. However, under no circumstances may this exception be invoked for the purpose of improving upon mediocre but playable shots, or of endeavoring to obtain by repetition a favorable outcome that could not be achieved through skill alone.

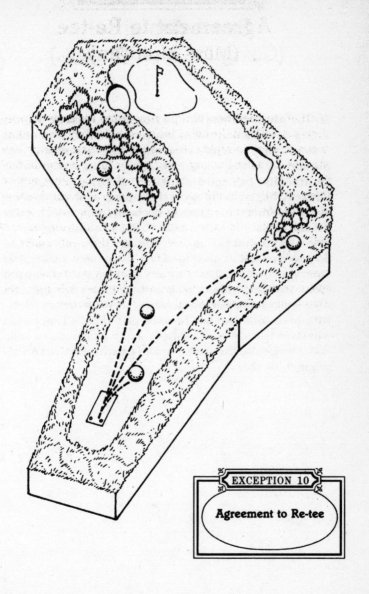

EXCEPTION 10

Agreement to Re-tee

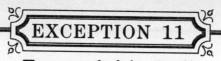

Expendable Ball
(Going for It on Doglegs)

On the teeing ground of any hole with a clearly defined dogleg layout, a player who wishes to attempt to hit a shot that takes a "shortcut" across unplayable ground and into the fairway may select and put into play a lower-priced or less desirable ball and declare that ball to be "expendable." If his drive then safely clears the hazards or obstacles occupying the intervening area of the bend in the hole, he may lift and replace it with a better ball and continue play. If, however, his shot fails to carry through to playable terrain, he may proceed at once to play a second ball without assessing a stroke or incurring any penalty, but he may not spend any time whatsoever searching for his first ball, and if he makes another unsuccessful attempt to "go for it" with his second tee shot, he must play that ball subject to whatever rules would normally apply and shall, in addition, be assessed the stroke and all penalties waived on his original tee shot.

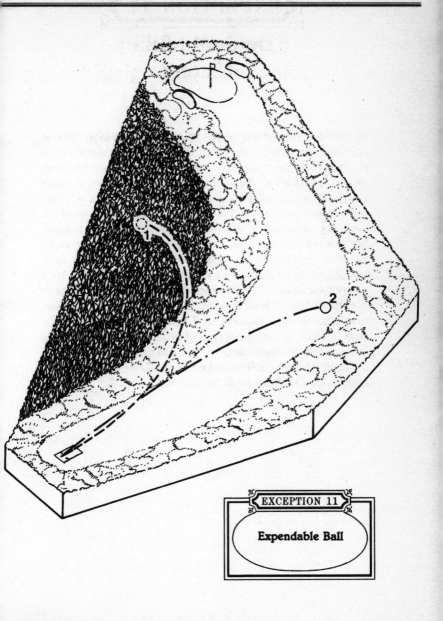

EXCEPTION 11

Expendable Ball

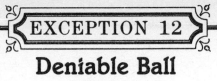

EXCEPTION 12

Deniable Ball
(Nixon)

If, owing to the unreasonable proximity of condominiums or other occupied dwellings along the boundaries of a course, a player shall, upon making a wayward tee shot, hear a splintering, cracking, or shattering sound, or some similarly alarming or worrisome noise, he may at once declare his ball to be "inadvisable to play" and immediately tee up and put into play in its place an "expedient ball" without assessing a stroke or incurring a penalty. However, during the remainder of his play on that hole, the player must behave as if his earlier misdirected shot never took place, and if he sees the affected homeowner or is confronted by him and betrays any awareness whatsoever that the mishap occurred, either by a verbal expression of apology or regret or a physical gesture indicating frustration, embarrassment, or discomfiture, then the stroke for his original errant drive shall be counted and all applicable penalties shall be assessed.

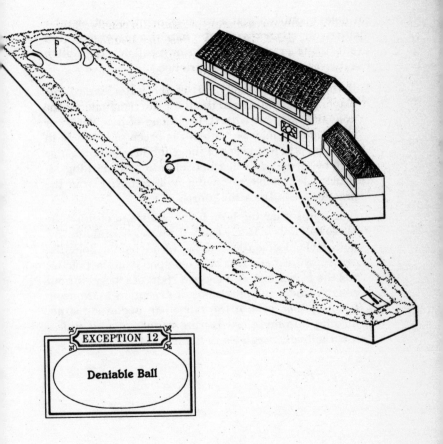

EXCEPTION 12

Deniable Ball

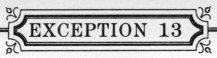
Junk Ball
(Milken)

On holes requiring that a tee shot be hit a considerable distance directly across a water hazard, a player may elect to substitute a range ball for his own ball, but this option is subject to the following restrictions:

1. If the range ball safely carries the water hazard, the player must continue to use it for the remainder of the hole and putt out with it, regardless of how flawed or misshapen it may be, unless the green of the hole in question is in plain view of the clubhouse and the range ball, by virtue of its distinct coloration or markings, is clearly identifiable as having been removed from the practice tee of the same course.

2. If, in spite of having been hit soundly and cleanly, the range ball fails to safely carry the water hazard due to a noticeable degradation of its aerodynamic potential caused by wear and tear inflicted upon it on the practice tee, the player may *not* claim a right of replay without penalty under the provisions of Exception 14, Nonconforming Shot, even if the range ball makes a distinct buzzing, humming, or whirring sound when hit, unless it actually disintegrates in flight.

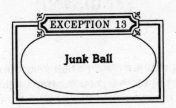

EXCEPTION 13

Junk Ball

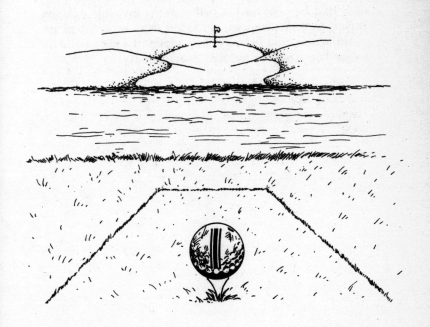

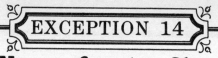

EXCEPTION 14

Nonconforming Shot
(Foul Ball)

If upon being struck a player's ball makes an oddly dead or flat sound, or produces a peculiar tingling or stinging sensation in his hands or fingers, or exhibits bizarre and surprising characteristics of flight, or travels in a direction or along a trajectory not typical of his normal style of play and not directly attributable to any known deficiencies in his game, or otherwise deviates so strangely and bewilderingly from the intended course in which it was propelled that the only possible explanation for the unprecedented mis-hit is that the ball itself was faulty, the player may state that he believes his ball suffered invisible damage during play or possessed a hidden flaw imparted in its manufacture, and he may then replay the shot without assessing a stroke or incurring any penalty.

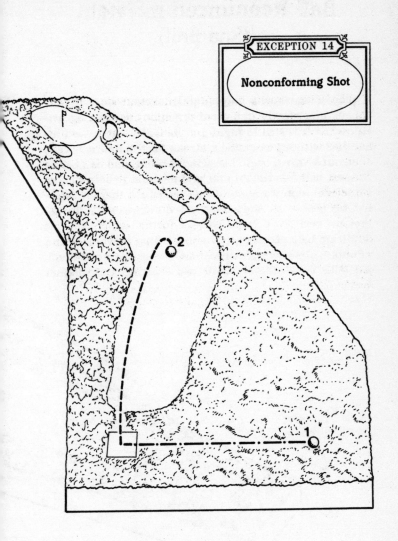

Ball Renounced in Flight
(Shapiro)

A player who hits a long, high drive that immediately travels in a clearly undesired direction may disown the ball while it is still in flight and instantly tee up and hit another without assessing a stroke for the first wayward shot, but he must begin his swing at the second ball before the first ball hits the ground, and he must remain in continuous motion throughout this procedure, thereby establishing that both shots took place during a single unbroken period of ball-striking during which he hit duplicate balls concurrently using a dual movement and a double-action swing, rather than hitting a pair of individual balls consecutively with two separate and distinct swings.

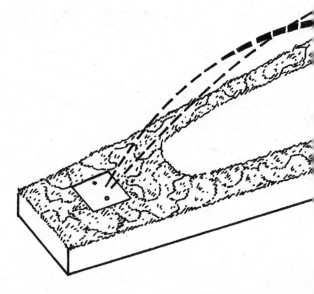

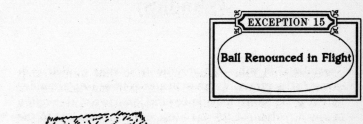

EXCEPTION 15

Ball Renounced in Flight

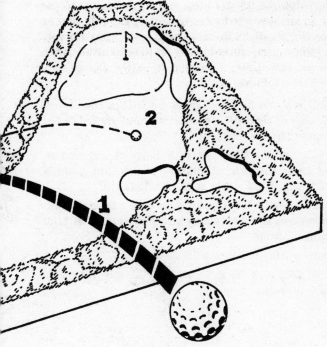

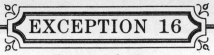

EXCEPTION 16

Casual Air
(Windies)

"Casual air" is wind of a volume or velocity sufficient to cause *(a)* a pinch of grass blades released at shoulder height to be blown a distance of at least two club lengths in any direction; or *(b)* the fabric bunting attached to the flagstick on any green to be drawn taut, or to ruffle, flap, or flutter, or the flagsticks themselves to bend, sway, or wobble; or *(c)* improperly affixed headgear to become airborne.

Whenever casual air is deemed to exist, players may obtain relief as follows:

1. The ball may be teed up anywhere within the closely mown area of the teeing ground without regard to the position of the tee markers.

2. Any ball hit out-of-bounds may be retrieved and replayed from the nearest playable lie within bounds, without penalty of either stroke or distance.

3. Any ball that flies unexpectedly far over a green, or falls conspicuously short of it, may be replayed once without assessing a stroke.

4. All third putts are conceded.

5. A range ball may be put into play at any time at a player's discretion.

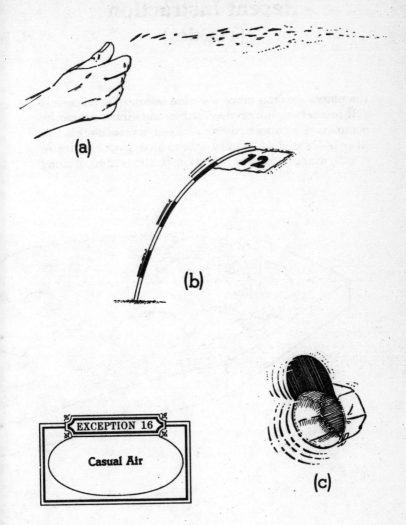

(a)

(b)

EXCEPTION 16

Casual Air

(c)

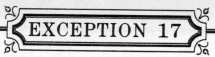
Recent Instruction
(Toskies)

If a player who has taken a formal lesson from a licensed golf teacher or club professional on the same day that he commences a stipulated round of golf approaches his ball in an oddly studied manner prior to hitting it, or addresses it with exaggerated concentration, or aligns himself along

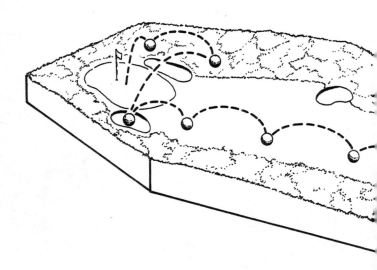

his target line with elaborate care, or waggles his club an excessive number of times, or interrupts his practice swing to examine the position of his elbows, arms, or upper body, or obsessively and repeatedly shifts the placement of his hands or feet, or noticeably alters the speed, plane, or length of his swing, or makes any other visible modifications in his characteristic style of play, and he then hits an unsatisfactory shot, he may replay it without assessing a stroke, provided that he clearly attributes the mis-hit to ineffective and inappropriate instruction and immediately abandons all of his recent innovations and returns to his traditional game.

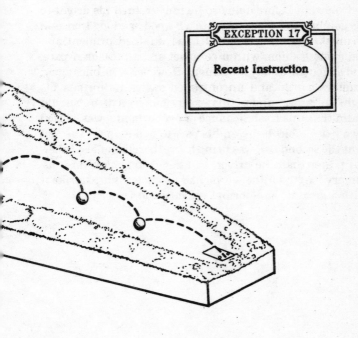

EXCEPTION 17

Recent Instruction

Temporary Insanity
(John Daly Drive)

If a player attempts to hit a drive an unprecedented distance through the use of an excessively long, fast, or forceful swing in which his torso is abnormally contorted, or his club shaft goes well past parallel in his backswing, or he audibly grunts or moans during the downswing, or either or both of his feet come out of his shoes at the conclusion of his follow-through, and the resulting shot is unsuccessful, he may tee up and hit another ball without assessing a stroke, but before doing so he must return his driver to his golf bag and replace it with a 3-wood or a long iron, and he must then swing that club in a restrained, prudent, and judicious fashion, with a compact arc, a measured pace, and a moderate body movement. However, if he once again employs a wild and uncontrolled swing, he forfeits his right to replay under this exception, even if he should claim that this fresh instance of overswinging was caused by a reasonable desire on his part to make up for the fact that the second ball was being hit with a club of less inherent power than the driver, and hence to achieve his customary length off the tee, he had no choice but to strike it with a greater-than-normal velocity and ferocity.

EXCEPTION 18

Temporary Insanity

IN THE
FAIRWAY

EXCEPTION 19

Providential Ball
(Found Ball)

If during an unsuccessful search for his ball a player shall find another ball that does not belong to him or to one of his fellow players and that does not appear to be currently in play from an adjacent hole, he may treat that ball as a "providential ball" and substitute it for his own ball if *(a)* it lies reasonably close to the point where he believes his own ball came to rest, *(b)* it is not an obviously different color, and *(c)* it is not a range ball.

In playing this providential ball, the player need not assess a penalty stroke, since the award of one minus stroke for having found a ball cancels out the penalty stroke for having lost his original ball.

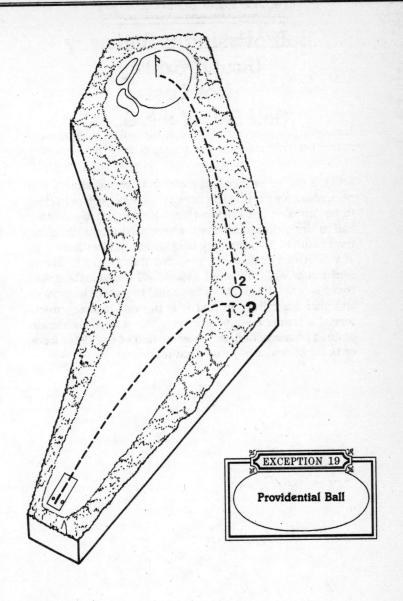

EXCEPTION 19

Providential Ball

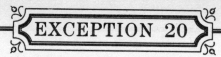

EXCEPTION 20

Ball Missing in Fairway
but Obviously
Not Lost
(Golf Ball of the Gods)

When a player cannot find a ball that he has clearly and unmistakably hit into the fairway, he may declare his ball to be "missing but obviously not lost" and drop another ball in the approximate place where his original ball must have come to rest, and play that second ball, without penalty of stroke or distance, provided that he is *absolutely and positively convinced beyond all reasonable doubt* that his original ball did in fact come to rest in the fairway and that his failure to find it is the result of the unobserved action of an outside agency, the effects of an unexplained phenomenon, the intervention of a sinister force, or the occurrence of a supernatural event.

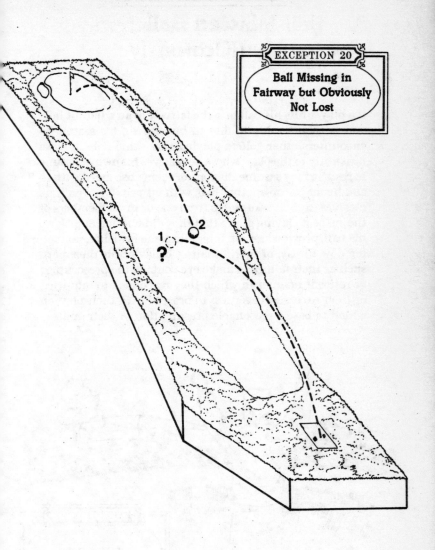

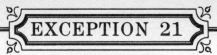

Stolen Ball
(Filchies)

If a player hits his ball into the fairway of an adjacent hole and is then unable to find it, but during his search he encounters other golfers playing that same hole in close proximity to the place where he believes his own ball came to rest, he may assume that one of them absconded with it, and he may drop another ball, without penalty, even if he receives explicit assurances from one or more members of the suspect playing group that they did not in fact pick up his ball, provided he can later cite some evidence, no matter how flimsy, of incriminating behavior on their part, such as their failure to make eye contact, the preoccupied or reticent manner in which they responded to inquiries, or their excessive eagerness to proceed with their play, on which to base a reasonable presumption of their guilt.

EXCEPTION 21

Stolen Ball

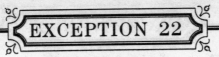
Unfairway
(Pete Dye Lie)

If a player hits a long, straight drive that comes to rest on closely mown turf in the middle of a fairway, but in a severe uphill, downhill, or sidehill lie, or on a knoll, knob, mound, or mogul, or in a bowl, scoop, hollow, dell, or gully, or among any other artificially shaped terrain features created for the sole purpose of improperly penalizing an impeccable shot, that player may kick or tap his ball, without penalty, to the nearest lie whose quality is more in keeping with the excellence of his shot. However, no ball, no matter how purely hit or foully punished, shall be deemed eligible for placement upon a tee.

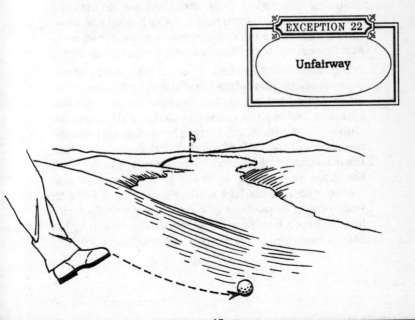

EXCEPTION 22

Unfairway

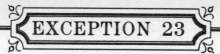

Preaddressing the Ball
(Mashies)

In the course of preparing to make a stroke in any place except a fair or formal hazard (see Exceptions 48 and 51), a player may take the following actions without penalty:

1. Prior to assuming his stance, a player who wishes to position himself in such a way that he can precisely determine his exact line of play by sighting along it may place his foot directly behind his ball, step solidly, and shift all his weight to that one leg, even if as an incidental consequence of this activity the turf or other ground lying immediately to the rear of his ball is compressed and the lie of his ball is elevated in relation to the surrounding area and thereby enhanced, but he may not rock back and forth from heel to toe or hop up and down unless he deems such movements essential for an accurate assessment of the distance or direction to his target.

2. Before addressing his ball, a player may, solely in the interest of safe play, press his clubhead into the turf or other ground behind his ball to probe for stones, roots, sprinkler heads, pipes, or the like that might damage his club or cause him injury during his swing, and test the soundness of the shaft of his club and the secureness of the attachment of its head by repeatedly tapping it on the grass or soil, and, in order to avoid cramps and undue strain in his legs while waiting for players in front of him to pass out of range, he may temporarily lean on his club in a resting posture as he stands by his ball in readiness to hit as soon as conditions permit.

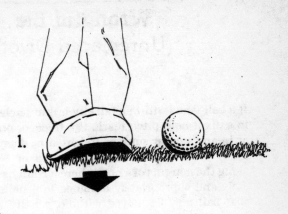

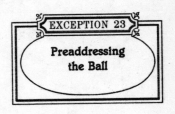

EXCEPTION 23

Preaddressing
the Ball

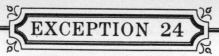

Wrongful Lie
(Unreplaced Divot)

If a ball lands within a fairway but unfairly comes to rest in a divot hole, pitch mark, tire track, or other concavity, or in any similar sunken, indented, or depressed lie more likely to be encountered in uneven or broken ground along the margins of a hole where terrain has been deliberately and appropriately designed to penalize errant play, that ball may be moved without penalty to the nearest adjacent lie where the condition of the playing surface is more nearly representative of the overall state of the turf generally prevailing throughout the majority of the fairway, when considered as a whole.

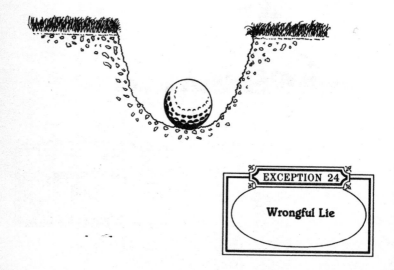

EXCEPTION 24

Wrongful Lie

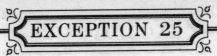

EXCEPTION 25

Ground in Need of Repair
(Munies)

If a player's ball comes to rest in a worn, eroded, or otherwise deteriorated area of a heavily played course, which, in his judgment, is clearly eligible for designation as "ground under repair" but has not been so marked due to an obvious oversight by the course maintenance staff, and where he feels that additional play would be likely to further degrade the already deplorable conditions, he may, without penalty, tap his ball to a playable lie in the nearest intact ground, provided that this action is *not* taken for the purposes of improving his lie but *solely* as part of a sincere attempt to protect damaged portions of the course from fresh injury.

EXCEPTION 25

Ground in
Need of Repair

Ground in Flight
Outdistancing Ball in Play
(Fat Shot)

If a divot taken at the time a ball is struck comes to rest at a point nearer to the hole than the lie ultimately occupied by the ball itself, that ball may be retrieved and replayed without assessing a stroke or incurring any penalty, provided that the divot is properly replaced.

EXCEPTION 26

**Ground in Flight
Outdistancing Ball
in Play**

Ball Played as It Once Lay
or Ought to Have Lain
(Ball Whistled Dead)

If a player's ball lands and comes to rest, however briefly, on the face of any slope, bank, or hill, and then, in a separate and distinct motion occurring after the completion of its forward movement, it rolls down the incline in a direction generally away from the green or toward or into a hazard or the rough, the ball may be lifted and replaced without penalty as near as possible to the point of its farthest advance.

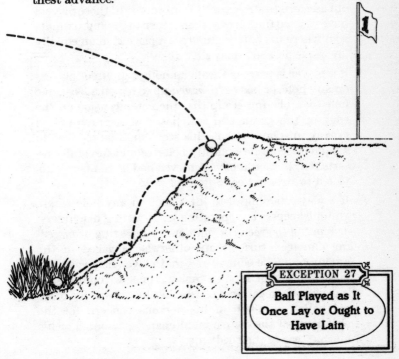

EXCEPTION 27

Ball Played as It
Once Lay or Ought to
Have Lain

Ball Hit Under Pressure
(Clutch Shot)

A player is entitled to relief when anxiety-producing conditions exist, as follows:

1. If a player hits his ball into an adjacent fairway, and players on that hole require him to make his next shot under their observation before they continue their play of that hole, and he then mis-hits his ball, he may either play it again from the place where it comes to rest without assessing a stroke, or he may wait until those players have vacated the fairway, then return to the approximate spot where his ball originally lay, place it in an equally favorable lie, and replay the stroke.

2. If a player is playing through another group of players on any hole, or has been waved up to hit on a par-three hole by a playing group that then stands aside on the edge of the green and watches, and he proceeds to grossly misplay the hole, his score shall be reduced to whatever score he honestly believes and forcefully asserts that he would have achieved had he not been subjected to stressful conditions of play.

3. If a player is obliged to hit a shot on any hole where groundskeepers are operating grass-cutting machinery, or tending to greens or bunkers, or repairing or reseeding damaged turf, or are otherwise engaged in the grooming of the course, and that player makes an unsatisfactory shot, he may replay it once without assessing a stroke, regardless of whether he mis-hit his original ball as a result of his nervous concern for the well-being of the course maintenance personnel or his morbid fear of their ridicule.

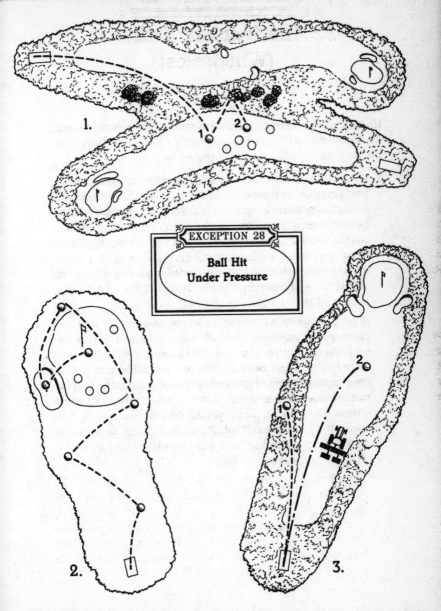

EXCEPTION 28

Ball Hit
Under Pressure

1.

2.

3.

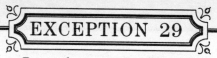

Inadvertent Ball
(Whoopsies)

If at any time during the play of a hole a player finds that he has accidentally and inadvertently hit a ball that does not belong to him, he shall proceed as follows:

1. If he is dissatisfied with his lie, or with the shot he hit just prior to his discovery that he played the wrong ball, or with any other stroke made thereafter, he may at that point immediately reveal the unwitting substitution with a suitable statement of regret for the mistake and delight at the timeliness of its detection and its coincidental mitigation of an unfavorable playing situation, and then, without penalty, play a ball of his own from a preferred lie on adjacent ground.

2. If he is satisfied with his lie and the shot he hit and his subsequent strokes on that hole, he shall continue, without penalty, to play the misappropriated ball as if it were his own, and he shall hole out with that ball, deferring until the teeing ground of the next hole the revelation of the unintentional misplay, which he shall then announce with an appropriate demonstration of distress over his error and relief that, due to the delay in its discovery, play on the hole was completed and thus the score he achieved may stand.

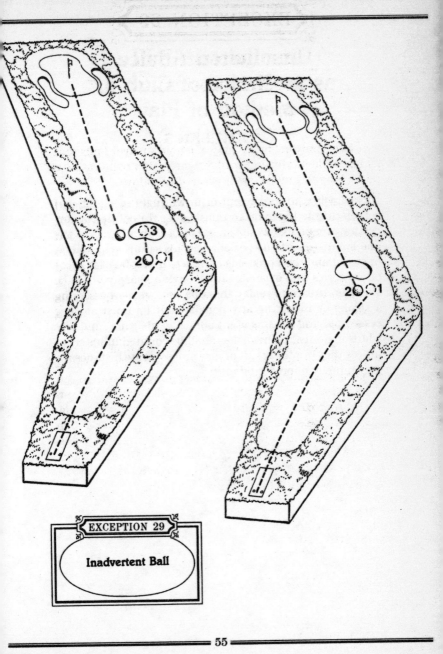

EXCEPTION 29

Inadvertent Ball

EXCEPTION 30

Unsolicited Advice as to Choice of Club or Method of Play
(Buttinskies)

Any player who, as a result of unwillingly receiving and reluctantly acting upon an unasked-for tip, pointer, or suggestion from a fellow player, selects a club other than the one he intended to use, or changes his set-up, grip, stance, or swing, and then proceeds to hit a ball that falls far short of or carries well over his target, or that sharply hooks or slices, is entitled to replay that one shot without assessing a stroke or incurring any penalty, but he must at once cease applying the unsought advice to his game, and any additional mis-hits he makes shall be counted in his score unless they are the result of new and separate instances of gratuitously offered guidance.

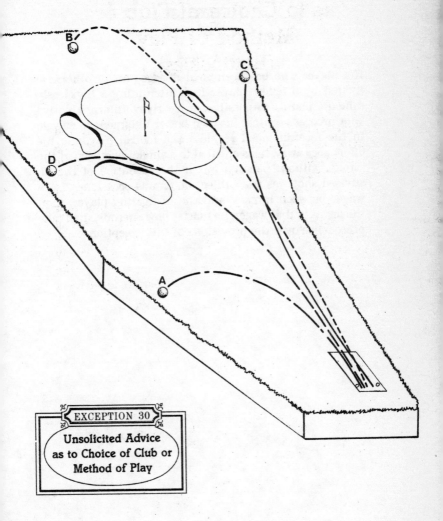

EXCEPTION 30

Unsolicited Advice
as to Choice of Club or
Method of Play

EXCEPTION 31

Preposterous Shot
(Goadies)

If a player who has been goaded, egged on, or otherwise incited by a fellow player into attempting a hopelessly difficult, plainly impossible, or clearly counterproductive shot proceeds against his own better judgment to engage in the recommended reckless and foolish play, and his effort goes awry, he is entitled to a single repetition of the stroke, without penalty, but if the execution of the ill-advised shot was the subject of, or was occasioned by, a wager between himself and the instigating player, then the terms of that wager, no matter how onerous, shall take precedence over the provisions of this exception.

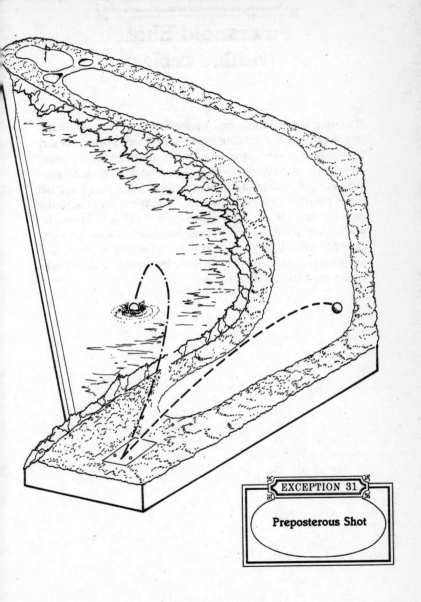

EXCEPTION 31

Preposterous Shot

Paranoid Shot
(Heebie-jeebies)

If upon addressing his ball a player notices that one of his fellow players is standing slightly in front of him, even if that player is well off to the side of the hole, far from his likely line of play, and out of his field of vision, and he elects to proceed with his play without requesting him to move and then mis-hits his shot, he may replay it without penalty, provided he states convincingly that the misplay was precipitated by an apprehension or nervous concern that his ball could conceivably hit that player, even if it would have required a stupendously errant or deeply peculiar shot to put him at risk.

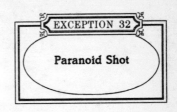

EXCEPTION 32

Paranoid Shot

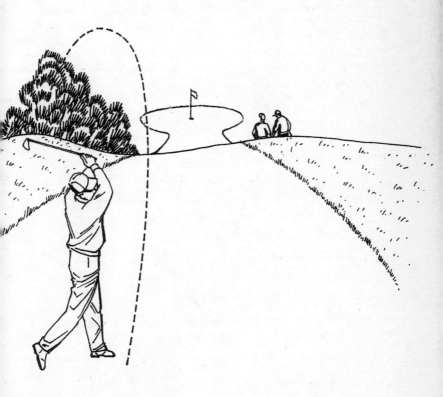

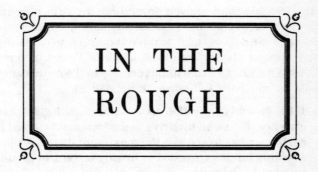

IN THE ROUGH

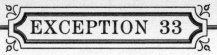

Unnecessary Rough
(Free Kick)

Any irregular and uneven ground having ruts, pits, and furrows, or expanses of excessively tall, deep, or dense grass, or clumps of thick stubble is deemed to constitute an improper playing condition, and a ball coming to rest therein may be kicked without penalty to the nearest playable lie under the following circumstances:

1. If the ground in question occupies the most logical place on a hole for a well-hit drive to land when it is aimed in such a way as to achieve the maximum distance while avoiding bunkers, wooded or brushy terrain, or ground lying out-of-bounds

2. If the ground in question occupies the only feasible position on a hole toward which a ball may be directed for safe play in the vicinity of a water hazard

3. If the ground in question lies within or cuts across a fairway or separates two sections of fairway from each other

4. If the ground in question occupies the part of a hole lying directly across the green from a deep or steep-sided bunker out of which a successful explosion shot is liable to be hit with excessive force

5. If it is clearly ridiculous to play out of the ground in question.

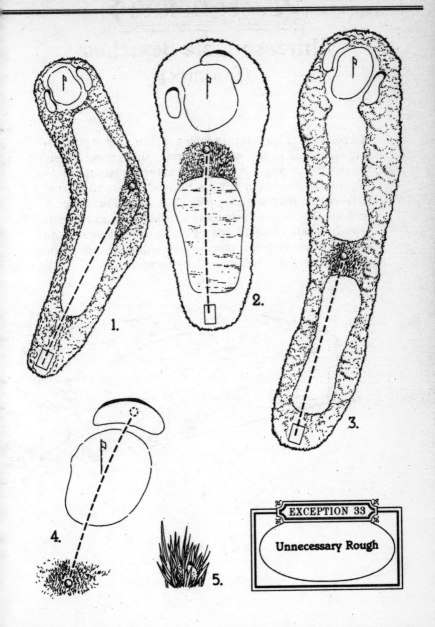

1.

2.

3.

4.

5.

EXCEPTION 33

Unnecessary Rough

65

Unreasonable Searches
(Boonies)

If a player hits his ball into a deep ravine, a steep gully, or any other wild or inhospitable terrain that appears likely to contain noxious or injurious plants or to conceal menacing animals, insects, or reptiles, he need not search for that ball, and he may, without penalty of stroke or distance, drop another ball in the nearest playable lie on an adjacent stretch of safe ground from which he can clearly see and point out to any fellow players the precise spot where he knows his original ball must have come to rest.

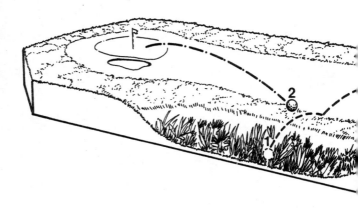

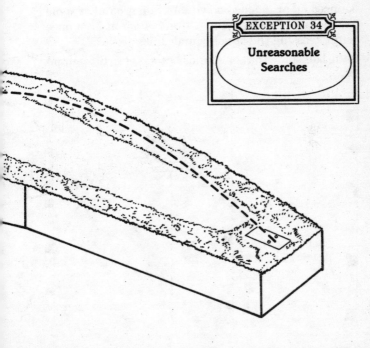

EXCEPTION 34

**Unreasonable
Searches**

Ball Hit Slightly Out-of-Bounds
(Just a Little over the Line)

A ball that comes to rest beyond the stakes, fencing, or lines defining ground out-of-bounds may be moved back within bounds and played without penalty of either stroke or distance under the following circumstances:

1. If the ball lies just beyond the line of the out-of-bounds stakes and can be tapped, pulled, dragged, or spooned back into bounds with any conforming golf club by a player standing within bounds

2. If the ball did not travel directly out-of-bounds but bounced off or touched down safely on ground or some fixed natural feature lying within bounds at least once before crossing the out-of-bounds line

3. If the ball landed out-of-bounds but was clearly attempt-

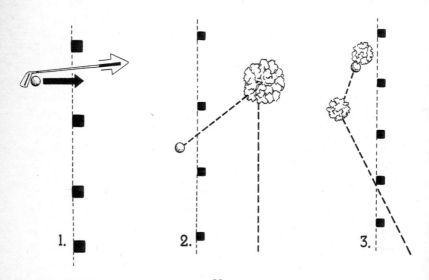

ing to return within bounds when its progress was improperly blocked by an impediment or obstacle located out-of-bounds and hence not a legal part of the course

4. If the ball has crossed an out-of-bounds line that is not a true course boundary but rather an administrative division of the ground lying between two adjacent holes drawn so as to discourage play from an adjoining fairway, and the player states that it was not his intention to engage in such play

5. If the ball lies within a portion of the out-of-bounds area that juts or bulges outward from the general line of the out-of-bounds stakes in such a way that if one or two of the stakes were removed, the remaining stakes would form a much straighter line that would leave the place where the ball came to rest well within bounds.

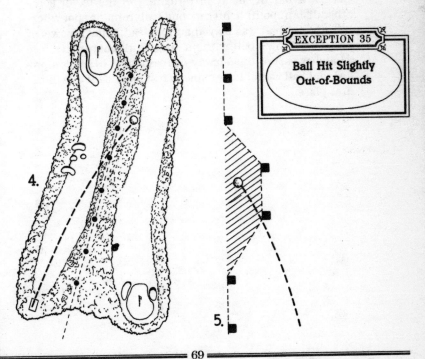

EXCEPTION 35

Ball Hit Slightly Out-of-Bounds

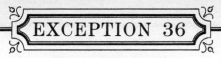

EXCEPTION 36

Provisional
Provisional Ball
(Powered Drop)

If a player hits a ball that he is confident he will be able to find or that he is certain remained within bounds, and he therefore decides not to hit a provisional ball, but then upon reaching the place where he knows it must lie he is nevertheless unable to find his ball or discovers to his surprise and consternation that his ball has gone deeply, totally, and indisputably out-of-bounds, that player may elect to avoid the delay of returning to the tee or some other distant point to hit a second ball from the spot where his original ball was played and instead make a powered drop and throw a ball, without any additional penalty, into whatever part of the fairway he reasonably believes a provisional ball would have come to rest had he hit one in the first place.

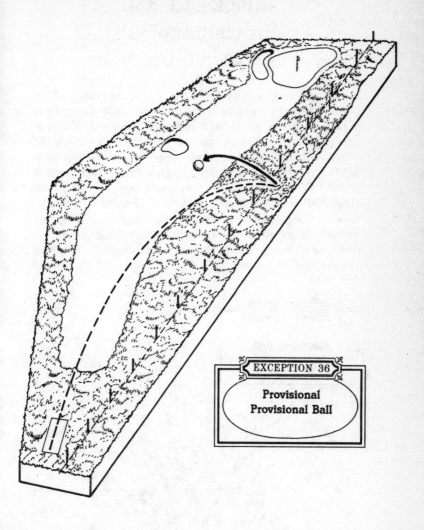

EXCEPTION 36

Provisional
Provisional Ball

Misplaced Ball
(Houdini)

If a player successfully finds his ball in extremely deep grass, a dense thicket, or some other absurdly overgrown portion of the course where visibility is severely limited, and then departs momentarily to retrieve a club with which to strike it, and upon his return discovers that he is unable to relocate his ball, the original ball is still deemed to have been found, but subsequently misplaced, and another ball may be dropped without penalty as close as possible to the place where the first ball vanished, but under no circumstances should it be permitted to come to rest in a lie so obscured from view as to run the risk of a second disappearance.

EXCEPTION 37

Misplaced Ball

Ball Hiding from Player
(Leafies)

If a player cannot find a ball that has been hit in plain sight into a reasonably playable area of the course where there is an accumulation of dead leaves, seasonal debris, grass clippings, or other forms of incidental camouflage in which a furtive ball could improperly conceal itself, the ball shall be deemed to be hiding, but not lost, and another ball may be dropped without penalty as close as possible to the place where the original ball is believed to be lurking.

EXCEPTION 38

Ball Hiding from Player

Botanical Obstruction
(Mushies)

When a player's swing is impeded by any part of a fixed
and growing plant, he may sit upon or lean against it in
order to address his ball provided that neither the assump-
tion of his stance nor the execution of his stroke results in
a permanent alteration in the shape of the plant or a significant reduction in its size.

EXCEPTION 39

Botanical Obstruction

EXCEPTION 40

Coincidental Demolition of Coarse Growth
(Weedies)

If a player's ball comes to rest behind a plant that is obviously a weed, or if the swing path his club must follow in order to fairly strike his ball is blocked by such a plant, the player may attempt to defoliate or dismember it with a series of practice swings, but the motions he makes with his club must be consistent with the movements golfers normally perform in the course of a swing, and they must be neither so numerous nor so violent as to appear to have as their sole and exclusive purpose the deliberate eradication of the plant.

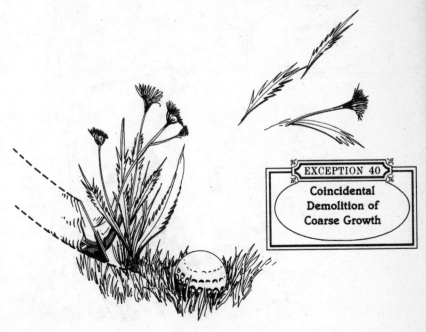

EXCEPTION 40
Coincidental
Demolition of
Coarse Growth

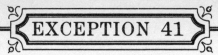

Removal of Deadwood
(Twiggies)

When a player's swing is obstructed by a twig or branch that gives every indication of being dead, he may break it off, but if upon being severed from its parent plant it turns out to have been alive all along, he must then immediately express chagrin and remorse, whereupon he may proceed with its removal in the interests of the continued health of the specimen.

Hostile Growth
(Thornies)

If, in order to sit upon or lean against a plant or remove deadwood from it or interweave and immobilize interfering branches, a player would have to subject himself to scratches, cuts, or pricks from thorns, brambles, briers, spines, burrs, needles, or thistles, he may, without penalty, tap or kick his ball to the nearest safely playable unobstructed lie.

EXCEPTION 42

Hostile Growth

EXCEPTION 43

Temporary Restraint
of Foliage
(Weavies)

If a player is impeded in the taking of his stance by a plant whose limbs or boughs are unmistakably alive but pliant enough to be bent and twisted without breaking, he may intertwine and interlace them in such a way that they remain fixed in place for the duration of his stroke, provided that the process of their immobilization does not require the use of artificial restraints such as belts, shoelaces, bag straps, or tag loops.

EXCEPTION 43

Temporary Restraint
of Foliage

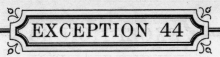

EXCEPTION 44

Unbelievable Ball Position
(Stymied Ball)

If upon locating his ball a player discovers that it has come to rest in a patently absurd lie or outrageously unplayable position under circumstances in which he is not otherwise entitled to claim relief, he may rectify the grossly inequitable playing condition, without penalty, by tapping, kicking, or throwing his ball to the nearest playable lie, provided he clearly states that if he is required to play his ball as it lies, he is likely to exhibit behavior not in the best interests of golf.

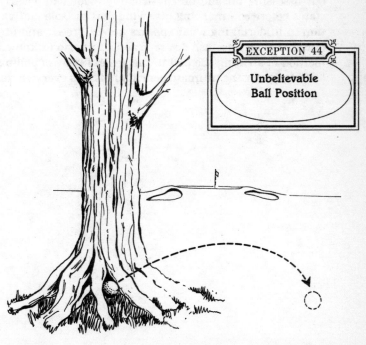

EXCEPTION 44

Unbelievable
Ball Position

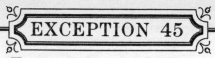

EXCEPTION 45

Experimental Shot
(Blind Stab)

When a ball comes to rest in a lie that precludes the execution of a conventional golf stroke, a player may elect to attempt an experimental shot incorporating an innovative manner of gripping or swinging the club or a novel means of addressing the ball. If as a result of this inventive and enterprising play the ball fails to move at all, or comes to rest in a position substantially worse than the one it previously occupied, he may then declare his ball unplayable and proceed to drop it in the nearest playable lie without assessing an additional stroke, provided he clearly states before commencing his swing that his sole motivation in undertaking what appears to be a greedy and idiotic shot is an unselfish desire to add a hitherto unknown method of striking the ball to the general body of golfing knowledge for the ultimate benefit of players everywhere.

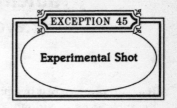

EXCEPTION 45

Experimental Shot

Suicidal Shot
(Kevorkian)

If a ball comes to rest in a playable but inherently perilous lie, such as on or among roots and rocks, on hardpan, in poison ivy or oak, up against the lip of a bunker, in uncommonly thick, wet, or tangled grass, on an unusually steep slope, or in a particularly deep divot hole, a player who sincerely believes that an attempt to play it as it lies could result in substantial physical harm may take advantage of his right to a therapeutic drop and move the ball without penalty to the nearest safely playable lie. However, before doing so, he must, in a clear and convincing fashion, and using appropriate medical terminology whenever possible, specify the particular portions of his anatomy that he feels would be subject to damage, and the nature and severity of the anticipated injury.

Note: This requirement is waived if, prior to the commencement of play on the first tee, the player in question has had the foresight to notify his playing partners that he is currently suffering from one or more preexisting physical impairments that would be seriously exacerbated by a misguided attempt to play a ball from a potentially life-threatening lie.

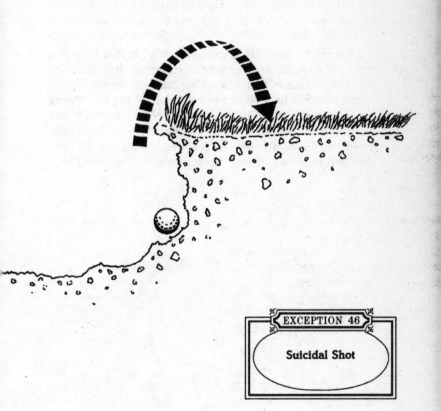

EXCEPTION 46

Suicidal Shot

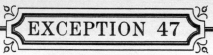

Adjustment of Lie Prior to Bold Play
(Arnie and Sevie Shots)

If a player declares his intention to hit his ball between, through, around, or over any obstructing objects, he is entitled, by reason of his dauntless and venturesome play, to improve his lie, without penalty, by rolling or tapping his ball to a perfect lie within two club lengths of his original ball position, but once having done so, he is obligated to attempt the shot he has designated, and he may not then make a safe play from his newly improved lie.

EXCEPTION 47

Adjustment of Lie
Prior to Bold Play

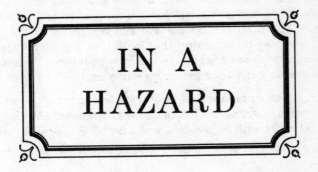

IN A
HAZARD

Cruel and Unusual Hazards
(Hellholes)

The following extreme water hazards and improper bunkers are deemed to constitute an unwarranted and impermissible interference with due and rightful play, and a player may replay a shot that is hit into any such water hazard, or throw his ball out of any such bunker, without assessing a stroke or incurring any penalty:

1. Any water hazard that, in order to be cleared, requires a ball to carry over it in the air for a distance of 150 yards or more with no possibility of a lay-up shot or safe play

2. Any lateral water hazard toward which a fairway has

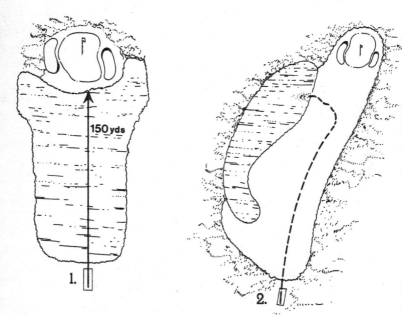

150 yds

1.

2.

been purposely graded or sloped so that a ball will roll or bounce into it even if, as a result of a benign spin or favorable curve applied to the ball at the time it was struck, it should have easily avoided the hazard

3. Any bunker so situated in a fairway that no part of it is visible from the teeing ground, regardless of whether the bunker was accurately depicted in a schematic diagram of the hole on a scorecard or sign

4. Any bunker having a lip of overhanging earth, turf, or greensward a foot or more in thickness, or a retaining wall of stone or wood a club length or more in height, or stairs or a ladder for entry or exit, or an overall depth such that the surface of the putting green is above the eye level of a player standing on the sand within it

5. Any bunker that has been formally given or is generally referred to by an ominous or intimidating name.

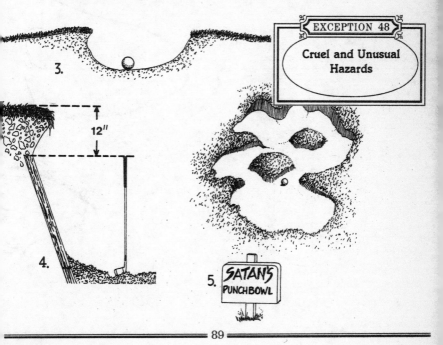

> EXCEPTION 48
>
> **Cruel and Unusual Hazards**

3.

12″

4.

5. SATAN'S PUNCHBOWL

EXCEPTION 49

Ball Playable in Water Hazard, but Just Not Worth It
(Sloppy Shot)

If a player's ball comes to rest within the margins of a water hazard in a highly playable lie from which he is certain he could, if he so desired, hit a successful recovery shot with no difficulty whatsoever, but the marshy,

muddy, swampy, or boggy state of the surrounding terrain makes it inevitable that in the execution of such a stroke, he himself, his clothing, or his equipment would be extensively soiled and/or soaked, or that he would be obliged to assume a stance requiring the time-consuming removal of his footgear or other elaborate preparations, he may move his ball, without penalty, to the nearest equally favorable lie inside the hazard where conditions are sufficiently dry to permit prudent, sensible, and reasonable play.

EXCEPTION 49

Ball Playable in Water Hazard, but Just Not Worth It

Environmental Hazard
(Ecologically Sensitive Shot)

If a player's ball comes to rest in ground within the margins of a hazard that has been deliberately left in a wild and natural state, *whether or not that area has been officially designated as an environmentally sensitive zone from which play is prohibited,* and the player in question has reason to believe that in making a swing he might damage rare, threatened, or delicate species of plants, or unduly disturb or traumatize endangered forms of animal life, he may drop his ball without penalty into an adjacent area of the course with limited biodiversity, such as a stretch of fairway with a monocultural planting of heavily fertilized hybridized turf grasses, where any moderate incidental destruction of nonnative vegetation that may occur during his shot is unlikely to have a significant negative impact on the global ecosystem.

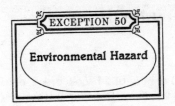

EXCEPTION 50

Environmental Hazard

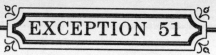

Informal Water
(Dry Water Hazard)

If, due to the seasonal drying of a brook, creek, or rivulet, or the diversion of a stream, or the evaporation of a pond during a prolonged period of drought, or the emptying of an artificial lagoon for regular cleaning, or an outflow from a marsh due to tidal action, or a scheduled release from an impoundment, or the draining of a reservoir, or a permanent and persistent state of desiccation in improperly designed or designated terrain, a water hazard fails at any time to contain a sufficient volume of actual, formal water physically standing or moving within its boundaries to cover at least one half of its total staked area, it ceases to be a valid water hazard and its status is automatically downgraded to "water nuisance." A player whose ball has come to rest on ground inside the margins of any such water nuisance may, without penalty, lift and clean his ball for purposes of identification, move loose impediments from it, and ground his club when striking it, or, if it lies in any remaining incidental water in the nuisance, he may remove his ball from that water and drop it in the nearest playable lie on dry and level ground.

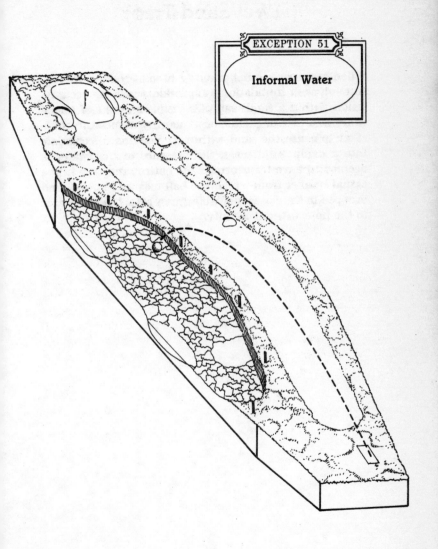

EXCEPTION 51

Informal Water

Casual Bunker
(Wet Sand Trap)

Whenever heavy rains, melting of snow or ice, leakage from pipes, or inundation by sprinklers cause an accumulation within a sand trap of a visible amount of casual water in a pool or puddle or a quantity of moisture sufficient to cause the sand within its margins to coagulate into a damp, solid mass, the presence of that water is deemed to have transformed the entire sand trap into a casual bunker from which the ball may be removed and dropped in the closest playable grassy area, but not nearer to the hole, without penalty.

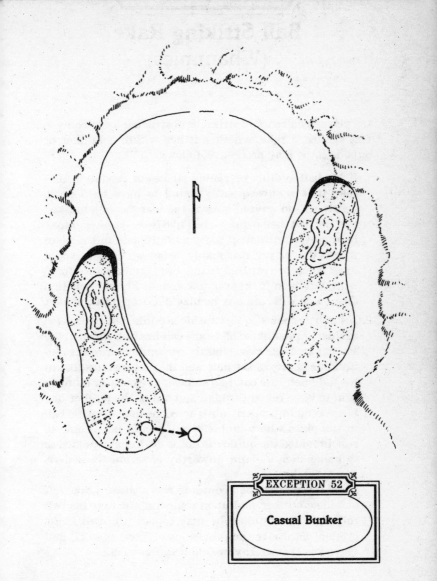

EXCEPTION 52

Casual Bunker

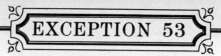

Ball Striking Rake
(Whammies)

If a player's ball should strike, be obstructed by, or come to rest against a rake, whether it lies within a bunker or outside it, he may proceed as follows:

1. If his ball audibly or visibly strikes or rebounds off a rake that is subsequently found to have been negligently left on ground outside the margins of a bunker, and the ball then comes to rest inside the bunker, it may be removed without penalty and dropped in the place where the player reasonably believes his ball would have come to rest had it not been unduly interfered with, but even if the original path of his ball was in a direct line with the pin, he may not drop it in the hole.

2. If his ball comes to rest inside a bunker but is lodged against or rebounded off a rake carelessly dropped in the sand at an angle even slightly perpendicular to the natural line of play of the hole, and the player states that in his judgment the ball had sufficient velocity or momentum to have rolled through and out of the bunker had it not been improperly obstructed, he may drop his ball in the place where he believes it would have come to rest, provided the bunker is not so deep or steep-sided as to make such a claim unworthy of serious consideration.

Note: If a player's ball comes to rest against a rake left outside a bunker, and upon removing the rake his ball rolls into the bunker, he may replace the ball in its original lie under the provisions of Exception 27, Ball Played as It Once Lay or Ought to Have Lain.

EXCEPTION 53

Ball Striking Rake

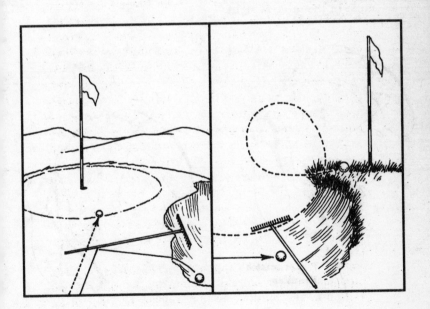

Equitable Stroke Control
in Bunkers
(Sandicap)

In order to ensure that an excessive number of faulty shots made in a bunker does not unfairly distort scores or unduly penalize flawed play in one small portion of the game, a player is required to throw his ball out of a sand trap, but not farther from the hole, once he has exhausted the full number of strokes allotted to him by his handicap for bunker play on any one hole, as specified by the formula in the table at right.

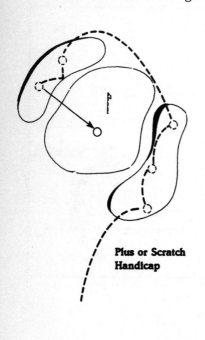

**Plus or Scratch
Handicap**

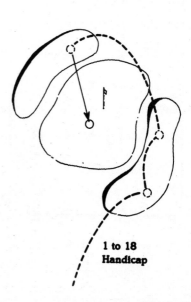

**1 to 18
Handicap**

HANDICAP	STROKE LIMIT IN BUNKERS
Plus or Scratch	No more than three strokes in any single bunker, and a total of no more than five around any one green
1–18	No more than two strokes in any single bunker, and a total of no more than three around any one green
19–36	No more than one stroke in any single bunker, and a total of no more than two around any one green
37–40	Remove all balls from any bunkers

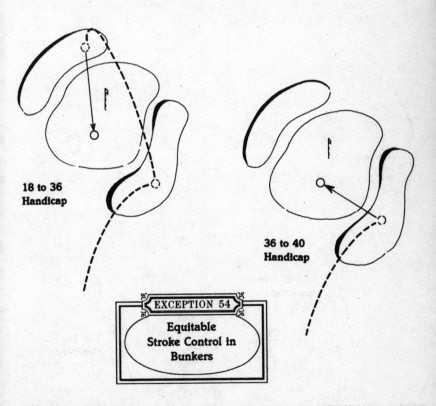

18 to 36 Handicap

36 to 40 Handicap

EXCEPTION 54

Equitable Stroke Control in Bunkers

ON THE
GREEN

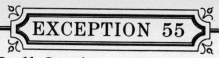

Ball Striking Flagstick
(Hitting the Pin)

If a player's ball audibly or visibly strikes any part of a flagstick properly inserted into the cup on a green, and the ball was hit from anywhere off the putting surface with a club other than a putter, and in spite of having squarely struck the pin the ball fails to enter the hole, that player is deemed to have holed out on the next stroke if his ball

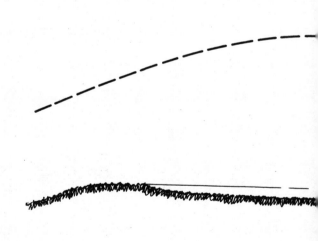

has come to rest reasonably near the hole, or in two strokes if it has come to rest in the fringe or grass surrounding the green, or on the green but a considerable distance from the hole. He may, if he wishes, for purposes of practice or amusement, attempt to make a shot conceded to him without being subject to forfeiture of the concession in the event he fails to sink it, but if he elects to do so he must play first, even if other balls lie farther from the hole, so that his fellow players have the opportunity to gain useful information from their observation of his unnecessary chip or putt.

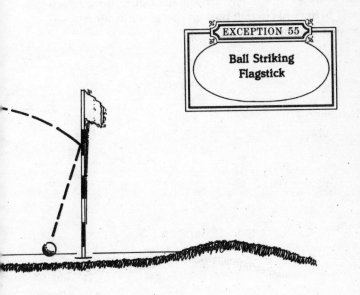

EXCEPTION 55

Ball Striking Flagstick

Punitive Pin Placement
(Impossible Putt)

On any sloping or undulating green where the cup has been deliberately located in relation to the hazards surrounding the green so as to force a prudent player to make an approach shot that leaves him with an excessively difficult putt whose misplay is likely to result in a substantial number of additional putts, that player may, without penalty, take one practice putt from the general position of his ball, but not along the exact line of his putt. However, if he elects to do so he thereby forfeits his right under Exception 57 to have his fourth putt on that green automatically conceded to him.

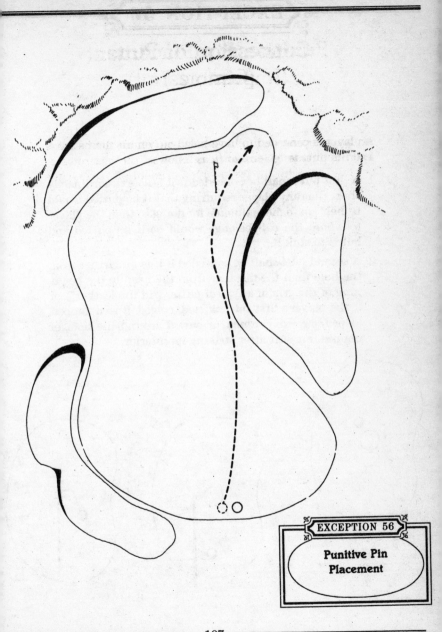

EXCEPTION 56

Punitive Pin
Placement

Concession of Putts
(Gimmes)

A player is conceded to have holed out on his next stroke, and his putt is "given," *only* as follows:

1. A first putt shall be conceded if it is so extraordinarily short that any player requiring that it be putted would be held up to more ridicule for doing so than the player to whom the ball belongs would be if he putted and failed to sink it.

2. A second putt shall be conceded if it is no farther from the hole than the distance from the head to the beginning of the grip of a typical putter ("in the leather"), or if the player's first putt skirted, ringed, lipped, lapped, looped, circled, rimmed, or curled around the hole, or hopped out of it after striking its interior.

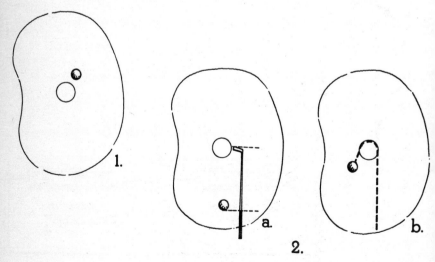

1.

a.

b.

2.

3. A third putt shall be conceded if it can be reached and picked up within one giant step by a player standing by the hole, or if that player reached the green in regulation but failed to sink his second putt for par.

4. A fourth putt shall be conceded if it lies anywhere on the putting surface unless the player took a practice putt on that green.

However, if a player attempts to hole out a putt that has been conceded to him and he fails to sink that putt, neither his next putt on that green nor any subsequent putts, no matter how short or how numerous, shall be conceded to him, but if his ball hit the flagstick on that green, this restriction shall be waived.

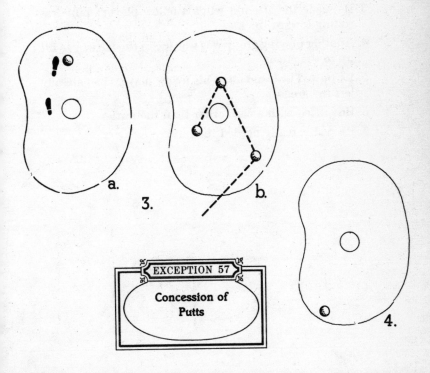

a.

3.

b.

EXCEPTION 57

Concession of
Putts

4.

EXCEPTION 58

Autonomous Concession
(Semi-gimme)

If a player misses an unconceded tap-in putt of four feet or less, he may retroactively give himself that putt, provided at least one of the following conditions has been met:

1. He played out of turn following a fellow player's suggestion that he putt out.

2. He adopted an awkward putting stance in an effort to avoid standing in the line of a fellow player's putt.

3. He made the attempt while a fellow player's putt was rolling toward the hole.

4. Another playing group was waiting in the fairway to hit up to the green.

5. He putted last, and all of his fellow players had already left the green.

6. He putted with a club other than the putter.

7. He really, really needed the putt.

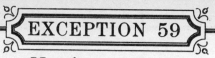

Negligent Putt
(Instant Re-putt)

If a player makes a hasty, tentative, or ill-considered stroke at a putt of six feet or less, and it is obvious from the moment the ball leaves the face of his putter that it will miss the hole by a wide margin, he may replay the putt, without assessing a stroke, provided he rakes the ball back to its original position before it stops rolling and then, reassuming his stance, conveys by the gravity of his demeanor and the painstaking deliberation with which he addresses the ball that, in sharp contrast to his earlier perfunctory and insincere effort, this re-putt will be undertaken with the unparalleled care and concentration that befits a serious attempt to propel the golf ball into the absolute dead center of the hole.

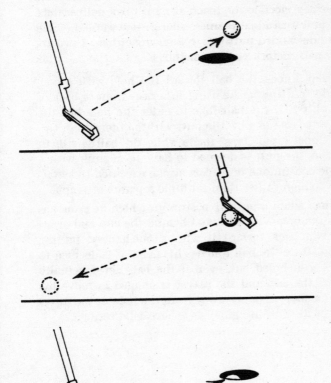

Nonchalant Putts
(Tap-tap-tap-in and Mittsie)

A player confronted with an unconceded putt of three feet or less may elect to approach the ball in a deliberately casual and unstudied manner and hit it toward the hole with a one-handed putting stroke using either of two approved perfunctory putting methods.

1. He may knock the ball toward the hole with a one-handed putting stroke using either the front or back of the putter. If the ball fails to enter the hole but the player is able to sink the putt with no more than two additional rapid "taps" made while the ball is still in motion, the putt is deemed to have been sunk with a single continuous multipart stroke executed in a staccato fashion rather than multiple separate attempts.

2. He may adopt a putting posture in which he crouches over the hole with his hand behind the cup and drags the ball back toward it with a one-handed pulling stroke. Once the ball touches his palm, it is deemed to have been holed out, even if the ball never actually enters the cup and the player is obliged to move his hand a short distance away from the hole in the direction of the oncoming ball to ensure solid contact.

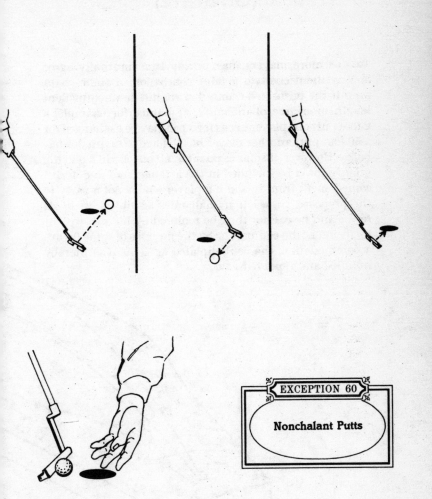

EXCEPTION 60

Nonchalant Putts

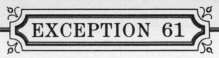
Negotiated Concessions
(Give-Give)

Two or more players may at any time mutually agree among themselves to a joint concession of their putts, even if the putts to be conceded are not of an equivalent length or degree of difficulty, and thus, for example, a 2-foot putt one player needs for a par may be exchanged for a 50-foot putt another player has to have to save a double-bogey. However, insofar as possible, all players in a playing group should be included in the arrangement and derive some benefit from it, and if a player who is not a party to the proposed transaction shall raise an objection to its terms and he cannot then be mollifed by his subsequent inclusion in the compact or by the promise of some future accommodation, the contemplated agreement is thereby nullified and rendered void.

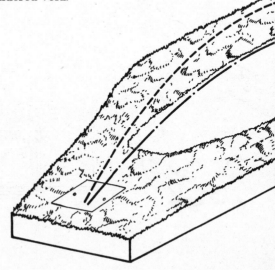

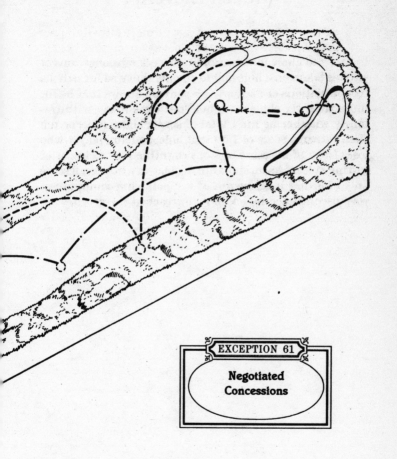

EXCEPTION 61

Negotiated
Concessions

EXCEPTION 62

Administrative Adjustment
of Scores
(Seven-Eleven)

In order to allow for occasional imprecise recollections of strokes taken on a hole and to obviate the need for tedious recapitulations of play, any player who knows that he hit more than six shots on a hole but cannot say with certainty whether he hit a total of seven, eight, nine, or ten shall return a score of 7 on that hole, and any player who loses track of his score or stops counting his strokes after hitting at least seven shots during play of a hole shall score an 11 on that hole, even if at the point his computation was discontinued he had not yet reached the green.

EXCEPTION 62

**Administrative
Adjustment
of Scores**

SPECIAL
SITUATIONS AND
LOCAL EXCEPTIONS

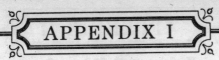

APPENDIX I

Course or Player in Substandard Condition
(Preferred Lies)

A player may place his ball upon a preferred lie in the fairway, the rough, or a hazard, without penalty, whenever any of the following conditions exists:

1. Ground Unfit for Strict Play by the Rules: When the playing surface of the course is in a generally unsatisfactory state due to winter frosts and freezes, spring thaws and inundations, summer heat and drought, or autumn leaf falls and storm damage

2. Ground Under Attack: When play is widely disrupted by the ravages of burrowing animals, an infestation of pestiferous insects, or an invasion by ill-tempered and untidy birds

3. Player Not Up to Par: When a player is experiencing discomfort from a currently occurring pain or preexisting injury, such as a strained back, an aching joint, a sore muscle, or a pulled ligament, which is likely to be aggravated by a bone-jarring stroke off a poor lie or a body-wrenching swing from an awkward stance

4. Player Under the Weather: When a player is suffering from allergies, bronchitis, or flu symptoms that may be exacerbated by dust kicked up by the impact of a clubhead on bare ground, or pollen or fungal spores dislodged by a stroke made through unmown grass in the deep rough, or a large volume of airborne sand particles dispersed by an explosion shot from a buried lie in a bunker, or a spray of potentially infectious vapor droplets produced by an attempt to propel a ball out of a wet lie in a water hazard.

APPENDIX II

Adverse Weather
(Winter Rules)

A ball may, without penalty, be rolled over to an improved lie in the fairway or placed upon a tee if no such lie is readily available, and tapped with a club back within bounds or out of the rough and into the fairway, and kicked away from all obstructions, and thrown out of all hazards at any time that one or more of the following conditions are deemed to exist:

1. The temperature is below 50°F (10°C), or there is a wind-chill factor equivalent to a temperature of 40°F (5°C)

2. There is any rain, drizzle, mist, or fog, whether intermittent or continuous, and any snow, sleet, or hail, whether presently occurring or previously deposited and not yet melted

3. Players have been obliged to don waterproof gear, insulating apparel, or any other restrictive garment that hampers or hinders their normal movements during play or interferes with their "touch" or "feel"

4. There has been a vocal expression of disbelief by non-playing onlookers that a round of golf is contemplated under the current circumstances

5. There is a general agreement among the players that play, given the prevailing weather, is indicative of an unbalanced mind or defective mental state.

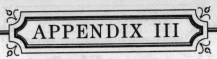

Unofficial Play
(Twilight Rules)

Whenever unofficial play is in effect and twilight rules are being adhered to, a revisional ball (mulligan) may be hit on every tee, all penalties for lost balls or balls hit out of bounds are waived, play from hazards is optional, and all second putts are conceded.

A player is entitled to engage in unofficial play as follows:

1. When he is playing at a reduced greens fee because of the lateness of his start

2. When he is playing a course for the first time

3. When he is playing with rented or borrowed clubs, or in tennis sneakers or running shoes, or without a golf glove

4. When he is playing an incomplete round or an accelerated round to take full advantage of remaining daylight, or is playing the holes of a course out of their correct sequence to avoid slow play

5. When sprinklers are in operation anywhere on the course

6. When he can no longer easily locate his ball because of increasing darkness or the glare of the setting sun

7. When he is playing alone.

APPENDIX IV

Unreasonable Delay
(Slow Play)

When the pace of play on any course slows to the point that the time required to complete a round of 18 holes exceeds four and one-half hours, the following variations from normal playing procedure may be observed:

1. On the tee of any hole where players were compelled to wait a significant amount of time before hitting, a first unsatisfactory drive is deemed to be a "warm-up" shot, and a second drive may be hit without assessing a stroke, but prior to the do-over the player must perform a few torso twists or back stretches or other muscle-loosening movements to demonstrate that an onset of stiffness occasioned by the prolonged pause in play was the immediate cause of the mis-hit ball.

2. If a player well back in the fairway of a par-5 or a long par-4 declines to hit to an occupied green, even though it would take a shot of unprecedented power and accuracy to endanger any of the golfers on that green, and then, when the hole is clear, he hits a shot that travels less than halfway to the green, he is entitled to replay it without penalty.

3. If, after watching a playing group on the green ahead take an unconscionable amount of time to putt out, a player then suffers a mental lapse that causes him to heel, toe-hook, shank, skull, or blade his approach shot directly at the departing group, he may drop another ball and replay the shot without penalty.

Unfamiliar Implements
(New Clubs)

For a period of six weeks following the purchase of new clubs, or during the first 25 rounds of golf played with those clubs, whichever shall come later, a player is entitled to the following relief:

1. A revisional ball (mulligan) may be hit on the tee of any hole as part of a conscientious program to "break in" a new driver.

2. Any shot that is significantly underclubbed or overclubbed or that travels in a genuinely unexpected direction may be replayed without penalty.

3. A shot that fails to slice or hook to the degree the player anticipated and allowed for and as a result enters a hazard, lands in deep rough or among trees, or carries out-of-bounds may be replayed without penalty.

4. No strokes shall be assessed for any swing in which a new club fails to contact the ball, or in which the club does contact it but the ball goes straight up into the air or directly into the ground, or the club makes a bizarre sound, or vibrates sharply, or flies out of the player's hands.

5. Any shot hit from a bunker with a new sand wedge that results in the ball traveling 20 or more yards farther than desired or a total distance of less than one yard may be replayed without penalty.

6. Any putt hit with a new putter that leaves a second putt that is as long as, or longer than, the first putt may be taken over.

APPENDIX VI

Resort Play
(Tropical Rules)

On any golf course in the Northern Hemisphere below 30° latitude, the following local rules shall apply:

1. The ball may be teed up in front of the tee markers or anywhere else on the teeing ground in order to take advantage of shade.

2. A ball hit into the ocean, onto a surf-splashed beach, or into any other saltwater hazard is deemed to have been mis-hit because of scenic distraction and may be replayed without assessing a stroke.

3. A player shall incur no penalty for declaring lost and abandoning a ball which, upon being struck into woods or undergrowth, elicited an animal cry.

4. No player shall at any time be required to play a shot from behind or beneath any seed, nut, or fruit-bearing tree.

5. Range balls may be put into play once a player has depleted his supply of good balls, or in an effort to stretch out that supply if no easily accessible source of reasonably priced replacement balls exists.

6. After twelve o'clock noon local time, a revisional ball (mulligan) is permitted on every tee, as all players then on the course are presumed to be driving while impaired.

Local Exceptions

Players desiring to remedy certain specific unfair playing conditions that prevail on a particular course should consider adopting one or more of the following local exceptions:

Tee Under Observation

Permitting an additional revisional ball (mulligan) on a tee other than the first tee of a course when the teeing ground in question immediately abuts an occupied dwelling, a business establishment, a school, a playground, a frequented road or sidewalk, or any other place where an unwanted audience might have the effect of causing a player to mis-hit a drive.

Municipal Play

Allowing the immediate concession of putts, the repositioning of balls, and alternate tee placements when, owing to the tightness of the course layout or congested, unskilled, or boisterous play, players deem themselves at any time to be at risk of being struck by balls hit from adjacent areas of the course.

Devious Terrain

Sanctioning the replay of significantly overclubbed or underclubbed shots on courses where deep fairway dips and dramatically elevated greens unfairly deceive players and cause them to consistently misjudge distances no matter how often they have played the course.

Vehicular Play

Stipulating that a player riding in a powered golf cart

that is confined by course rules to a mandatory cart path may, without penalty, throw his ball out of a lateral water hazard, ground out-of-bounds, or deep rough lying anywhere near the cart path so long as he has made it clear that the only reason he hit his ball in that direction was because he wished to avoid exhausting treks and imprecise club choices caused by safe but inconvenient ball positions.

Visual Interference

Authorizing an upward adjustment in the handicap of a player compelled to play in the company of golfers wearing sporting attire characterized by violently discordant color combinations or egregiously inharmonious patterns.

Decorative Plantings

Declaring that on courses where flower beds, ornamental shrubs, and other inappropriate forms of purely decorative landscaping have been installed to the detriment of play, any ball that comes to rest in or which is blocked by a horticultural impediment may be moved without penalty to the nearest playable lie.

Hackneyed Utterances

Imposing a one-stroke penalty on a player every time he uses the phrase "Show us how it's done," "That'll play," "Knock it close," "Never up, never in," "Does your husband play golf?" or "What's the matter—did your putter get caught in your skirt?"

Gastric Distress

Establishing that a player who made imprudent food or beverage selections at a snack bar at the turn has the right to replay any shot on the back nine that is preceded or accompanied by audible evidence of indigestion.

Basic Techniques
for Improving
Your Lie

Rolling the Ball Over: This is the best method to use when your ball is sitting down in the rough or in a divot hole in the fairway. Use the head of the club to pull or push the ball onto the nearest level patch of turf. Don't try to nudge it onto the top of a perfect tuft of grass. It's probably going to start to roll off halfway through your backswing, and even if you do manage to get it to stay put, the odds are you'll sky your shot.

Rolling Over

Tapping the Ball: When your ball is under a shrub or in thick undergrowth and it's awkward to kick it or pick it up, your best bet is to knock it into a playable lie using a short, one-handed chopping motion with a club. This is no time to think about getting it into the middle of the fairway. Just concentrate on popping your ball out into the open where you can make an unobstructed swing, and use that stroke you just saved to put yourself into a great position for the next shot.

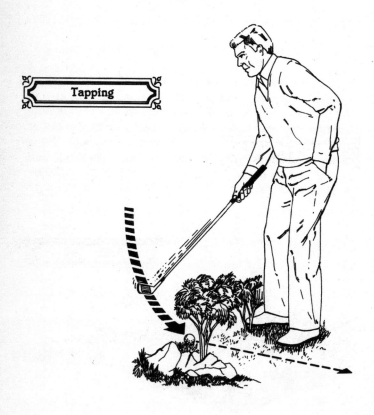

Tapping

Kicking the Ball: If your ball ends up on hardpan or a bare, stony patch of ground or on a road or path that's part of the course, you're better off kicking it into an adjacent grassy area than tapping it there with a club. For one thing, you won't risk nicking your club head or hurting your wrist if you happen to strike a rock, and you're much less likely to accidentally hit the ball too hard and send it hopping into some other equally bad lie 20 or 30 yards away.

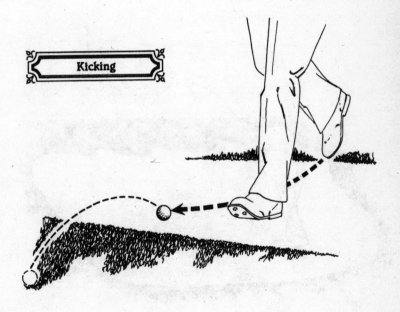

Kicking

Throwing the Ball for Accuracy: Any time you're trying to toss your ball to a specific spot, whether you want to bowl it out from deep in the woods or lob it from a hazard and onto the green, the key word to remember is *touch*, not *muscle*. Choose a target you know you can reach easily, and keep your eye on it throughout your throw. Use an underarm pitching motion, and don't get fancy. Putting spin on the ball or attempting a complicated trick shot is asking for trouble . . . and trouble is what you want to get *out of*, not *into*.

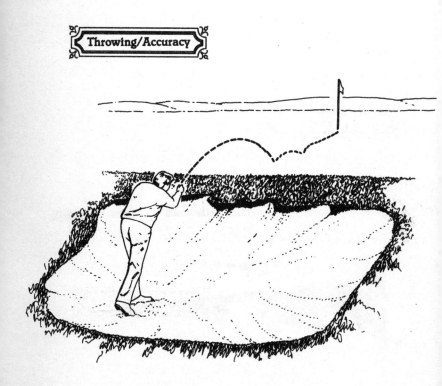

Throwing/Accuracy

Throwing the Ball for Distance: Whenever your ball ends up in a totally unplayable area of the course or way out-of-bounds, there's really only one thing you can do—throw it overhand as hard and as far as you can. But take a moment after you pick up your ball to decide whether you are going to try to get it as close to the hole as possible or into as good a lie as possible. You probably can't have both, and if you don't make up your mind before you make your throw, you may end up with neither.

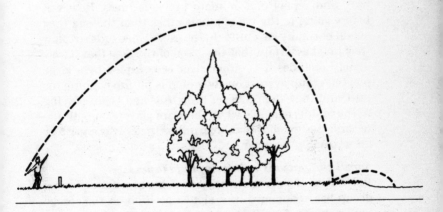

Throwing/Distance

Commonsense Etiquette

Discourtesy on the Course

Cutting In

A group of players that is frustrated by the continuous refusal of a slower group in front of them to wave them through may go around them and proceed to another hole, even if it is not the next hole in order of play, or cut across to another hole, even if it is not a part of the same nine-hole portion of the course currently being played, or loop back and replay one or more previous holes. However, before going to the tee of a hole other than the one they would normally encounter in the established order of play, they must ascertain that the green of the hole that immediately precedes it is either clear or occupied by a large playing group at least one of whom is plumb-bobbing his putt, and they should never drop balls and begin playing in the middle of a hole when there are players on both the tee and the green of that hole, unless the hole is a par-5 or an unusually long par-4.

Moral Obligations of Interloping Players

Regardless of their motivation in doing so, once a playing group has abandoned its assigned position on the course and insinuated itself at some other point in the progression of holes, the members of that group are under a special obligation to insure that they themselves do not delay the play of other golfers occupying their rightful places, but if they are challenged as to their legitimacy by another playing group that believes itself, rightly or wrongly, to have been inconvenienced by their actions, then, in the interests of maintaining harmony on the course, it behooves the intruding group to lie outright as to the validity of their status.

Reckless Play

If a player thoughtlessly hits a ball into the playing group in front, a member of that group may pick up the ball, or hit it into a hazard, deep rough, or the woods, or step on it, or drive over it with his cart, but he should not attempt to hit it back at the perpetrating player unless the offense was particularly egregious and he has sufficient confidence in his ball-striking abilities to insure that his shot does not result in personal embarrassment or the accidental injury of an innocent player in an adjacent fairway who has no inkling that he is at risk of being struck by a golf ball hit from a completely unanticipated direction.

Throwing Clubs

A player who feels compelled to display his dissatisfaction at the outcome of a shot by tossing, casting, or hurling the offending club should employ a simple overhand "tomahawk" motion that drives the club directly downward onto or into the turf, rather than a body-driven sidearm "windmilling" action, which can propel the club a considerable distance in a dangerously unpredictable direction.

Equipment Left on the Course

If a player happens upon a club, club-head cover, or similar item left behind on the course by a player in a group that previously played the hole, he should endeavor to return it as soon as practicable, but if it was mislaid by a member of an intolerably slow playing group immediately ahead, he may, before reporting the find, first ask that group to allow him and his fellow players to play through, and if permission to do so is withheld, he may then dispose of the recovered equipment in any way he sees fit.

Priority on the Course

A match composed of players who appear to be armed, or to have criminal backgrounds, or to be pursuing careers in professional team sports or law enforcement, or who are visibly intoxicated or clearly insane, has precedence over any other match, which should invite them to play through without delay.

Care of the Course

Prompt Repair of Damage

In order to insure that the distraction of observing and evaluating their shots does not cause players to neglect their duty to repair any damage to the course that they may encounter during their play of a hole, all footprints in bunkers should be raked smooth, all divots replaced, and all irregularities on greens tamped down *both before and after* the shot is played, even if the remedial action has the coincidental result of substantially improving a player's lie or positively affecting the outcome of his shot.

Destruction Caused by Displays of Emotion

Physical expressions of disappointment and disgust at the outcome of a shot, such as kicking the turf or striking, chopping, hammering, or stabbing it with a club, should be confined to the deep rough or ground within the margins of a hazard, and tree trunks and limbs used as points of impact by a player seeking to deform or demolish a club should be of sufficient heft and girth to withstand the force of the blows without suffering permanent harm.

Golf Carts

Local regulations restricting the movement of golf carts to particular areas of the course or to cart paths should be strictly observed whenever players are in view of the clubhouse.

Index

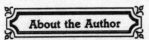

About the Author

HENRY BEARD was a founder and one of the original editors of *National Lampoon*. He is the author of a number of bestselling humorous books, including *Miss Piggy's Guide to Life, French for Cats, Poetry for Cats, Latin for All Occasions, O.J.'s Legal Pad* (with John Boswell), and *The Official Politically Correct Dictionary and Handbook* and *The Official Sexually Correct Dictionary* (with Christopher Cerf). He is also the author of several golf classics, including *Golfing: A Duffer's Dictionary, Mulligan's Laws,* and, with Leslie Nielsen, *Leslie Nielsen's Stupid Little Golf Book* and *Leslie Nielsen's Bad Golf My Way*. He drew on four decades of remarkably erratic play to assemble and codify the many special exemptions and extenuating circumstances in the Special Titanium Edition of *The Official Exceptions to the Rules of Golf,* and as part of his ongoing research into the finer points of the regulations governing the game, he is out on the links virtually every day. Yes, it *is* hard work, but somebody has to do it.

The World's Best Golf Jokes

Robert McCune

Whether you're a brilliant professional, an enthusiastic amateur or a golf widow, there's something for everyone to chuckle at in this hilarious collection of *The World's Best Golf Jokes*.

Side-splitting, saucy and entertaining, this book is a must for anyone who knows anyone who plays the ever-popular game of golf.

'I'd move heaven and earth to be able to break 100 on this course,' sighed the veteran.
'Try heaven,' advised the caddie. 'You've already moved most of the earth.'

'What's your golf score?' the country club interviewer asked the prospective new member.
'Well, not so good,' replied the golfer. 'It's 69.'
'Hey, that's not bad. In fact, it's very good.'
'Glad you think so. I'm hoping to do even better on the next hole,' the golfer confided.

0 00 638332 7

Latin For All Occasions

Henry Beard

Who says Latin is a dead language? The Roman mass may be a thing of the past, but Latin's never been livelier.

Henry Beard, former prisoner of the classics, has produced an essential tool for anyone who's ever struggled with an ablative. Here, in one handy volume, are hundreds of everyday English expressions rendered into grammatically accurate, idiomatically correct, classic Latin and an easy to use pronunciation guide.

Latin For All Occasions gives you the perfect phrase for every contemporary situation from starting a relationship (*Frequentasne hunc locum?* Do you come here often?) to making a swift exit (*Di! Ecce hora! Uxor mea me necabit!* God! Look at the time! My wife will kill me!)

'Humour book of the year' – *The Times*

ISBN 0 00 255383 X